Surviving the
BADGE

A Woman's Struggle of Saving Her Son
& Protecting Her Community

Irene Reyes-Smith

Publishing Services: Pen Legacy®
Cover Designed By: Christian Cuan
Editing and Typesetting: Carla M. Dean of U Can Mark My Word

Library of Congress Cataloging – in- Publication Data has been applied for.

ISBN: 978-1-7370120-2-3

PRINTED IN THE UNITED STATES OF AMERICA.

Victory Is Mine

I wish I were the mom that my mother was, but I managed to mirror her ideas, thoughts, and accomplishments. My life is great, and despite my trials, triumphs, and tribulations, God has been with me through it all! God is amazing, awesome, and all I've ever needed. He is my rock, my strength—whom shall I fear?

This is ME, Irene Reyes-Smith. I dedicate this book to the late Ana Redman Reyes and Jose G. Reyes, my parents whom I adore and love so much. You will forever be in my heart. Thank you for all you have taught, nurtured, and instilled in me to keep God first in all that I do.

Table of Contents

Surviving the
BADGE

A Woman's Struggle of Saving Her Son
& Protecting Her Community

Preface

I am a Washingtonian, born on September 8th—a summer baby set apart by God to be great and covered in a peaceful spirit. As a teen, I accepted the Lord, triggering a journey filled with joy, challenges, pain, and abundant blessings. Through it all, I trusted Jesus, and the enemy has fallen off. The Lord has declared the storm is over; I will receive double for my trouble. You're about to read a firsthand account of how the devil tried to stop me. However, God was enough. He had my back and helped me to press on.

How Did I Fail My Son?

The sight of my son dressed in a standard orange prison-issued jumpsuit made my heart drop. Tears burned my eyes, but I refused to cry. I needed to stay strong and shield him from the impact his incarceration had on my life. Like a bad dream I couldn't wake up from, I dreaded the end of our visit and being forced to walk away from my son. Once I exited the doors of the facility, I allowed the tears to fall freely down my face. My life, as I once knew it, changed.

Seeing my son confined to a cell like an animal shattered my heart. Even though I tried to remind myself that many other mothers had dealt with my new reality, I couldn't come to grips with the pain. As I drove away, I prayed, "Lord, help me assist young men trapped in this way of life. Most importantly, help me save my son."

In the Beginning

September 1969 — a baby girl, the fifth of six siblings, was born to parents of Hispanic descent. My mother was a religious woman who taught her children to believe in God and pray. We were an imperfect but God-fearing family. Once I was of school age, I balked at being required to learn English, which I did not think was cool at the time. My childhood was challenging, but we learned the importance of making our way. Our parents embedded the customs and values of our culture into us at a very early age. We understood that we had to work hard for what we wanted and to put family first always.

Trying to be American while preserving my Hispanic heritage was hard, but I managed to maintain a normal childhood. I was the girl who always wanted to make a difference in whatever situation I was faced with, but I often talked too much. What can I say? I had the gift of gab and asked questions. My mother once told me that we have to ask questions if we want to know something, which I did to the fullest. I remember one incident in sixth grade when I had finished all my work. The teacher had already told the class no talking was allowed, but I loved to talk! When the teacher asked why I was talking, I responded, "Because I finished my work, and God gave me this mouth!"

My response got me kicked out of class and sent straight to the principal's office. I was so nervous, wondering what I had gotten myself into. Not wanting my parents to find out, I called my sister, Josefina, and explained what happened. She came up to the school and got me back in class, but that was just the start of my mouth being the cause of bigger problems.

In junior high school, my mouth got me into more trouble and fights. My two best friends, Lisa and Nicole (who were more like my sisters), warned me that my mouth was going to get all of us into trouble one day. I calmed down for a while but eventually went right back to my destructive ways. Although I was often in the wrong, my friends had my back. One evening when I was out with Lisa and Nicole, I dropped the news that I wanted to become a police officer.

"What??? A police officer?" they exclaimed in unison.

"Yes, a police officer," I reiterated with an attitude.

They giggled and replied, "With that mouth? You're going to get everyone hurt."

"Be quiet," I snapped, then we fell into a fit of laughter.

As I got older, I developed a passion for helping others, as I had always seen my mother do. But first, I knew I had to change my life. One evening during church, the preacher called for souls to come to Christ. Not knowing what to expect by accepting the Lord, I nervously dragged myself to the altar. A powerful feeling washed over me that I believe was Christ's presence. From that day, I put my childish ways behind me and allowed the Lord to lead my steps.

Upon graduating from high school in 1987, I decided to pursue a law degree and enrolled in the University of the District of Columbia. However, since I didn't have much support or push to stay in college, I became uninterested in putting in the work to reach my goal. As my displeasure became noticeable, my baby brother, Tony, had several talks with me about my education.

"What are you going to do? Are you going to finish college or play around?" he demanded to know.

Even though I heard him speaking, unfortunately, I was not listening. Instead of focusing on my studies, I began hanging with the wrong crowd, cutting class, and being irresponsible.

Ambitious and independent, I began working at Ames Department Store as a cashier at the age of nineteen. Soon thereafter, management promoted me to a front-line CSM (customer service manager). A year later, during one of my shifts, it hit me that there had to be more to life than what I was doing.

One day, I approached Officer Wiley, who worked at the store part-time, and inquired about becoming a police officer. I had never abandoned that original dream. He told me about the Metropolitan Police Department's Cadet program, which recruited young adults who had graduated from high school and were under the age of twenty-one. I looked at the program as an opportunity for me to escape a dead-end job and better myself.

The next time I ran into Officer Wiley at the store, he handed me an application to fill out and told me where to return it. I thanked him profusely; I was ready to change my life. The following day, I began the process and was on my way to achieving my childhood dream. I remained at Ames until everything was finalized. Then I turned in my two weeks' notice in preparation to start my new journey.

In April of that year, I prayed to God, "Lord, I know Your plan isn't for me to work at someone's department store for the rest of my life," to which God responded, "Be still and know that I am God. Whatever I say will come to pass." In that moment, I knew to continue trusting the Word of God.

A few months later, I received a phone call with wonderful news. I had been accepted as a cadet in the Metropolitan Police Department. "Thank you, Lord!" I screamed. The joy I felt when I got that call, the world didn't give me and certainly couldn't take it away. I was about to become the police officer I always wanted to be!

Happy, excited, and honored, I started the cadet program at twenty years old. My mother was happy for me, too, but couldn't help being nervous.

"Are you sure this is what you want to do?" she asked.

"Yes, Ma," I assured her with confidence.

My father, on the other hand, didn't ask many questions

about my career choice.

"If that's what you want to do, just be careful," he told me.

Moving forward, I graduated from cadet, to recruit, and finally, to officer.

The Mighty Blue

The academy was a challenge, but I managed to navigate my way through. All the studying, training, and testing kept me busy, but every bit of it was worth it. At the academy, I met a young lady named Tiffany, with whom I became best friends. After all the long days, intense workouts, and exasperating challenges, I finally graduated and was assigned to the Fifth District Police Station.

In the year 1990, elevated levels of extreme violence, crime, and drugs plagued Washington D.C., the nation's capital, referred to as the *"murder capital"*. Yet, there I was giving birth to my dreams while being surrounded by homicides. I was assigned to Montana and Saratoga Avenues, an area known for high crime rates and drugs. This prompted my mother to pray for God's protection and provision over my life. Every evening, I came home and shared the stories of patrolling the streets of D.C. with my family. My mother was so scared that she would admonish me daily to be careful.

Irene Reyes-Smith

In 1991, after one year of serving in the department, I discovered my baby brother was dealing drugs. He wanted shoes, clothes, and other expensive things my parents would not purchase for him. Tony loved the finer things in life, but his job didn't pay enough for him to afford what he wanted. So, I began purchasing shoes for him to keep him out of trouble.

Being a praying woman, my mother asked God to deliver my brother from the street life. "You're crazy involving yourself in this, knowing your sister is a police officer," she scolded him. That was the start of the enemy attacking what God had already predestined in me. Of course, my mother had already warned me what was going on, so I prayed — knowing where two or more are gathered together in His name, the Lord is present.

God reminded me to *"trust in the Lord with all your heart; do not depend on your own understanding. Seek his will in all you do, and he will show you which path to take. (Proverbs 3:5-6, NLT)*

One evening, my brother and I were out on the porch talking. At the time, I was twenty-one years old, and he was twenty. I wandered back into the house to get some water, leaving him alone. Suddenly, there was screaming outside. Someone had pulled up and tried to kidnap him! I bolted from the house; some of our neighbors did, too. We hollered at them, and they released my brother as we chased them away. My brother, shaken and scared, was happy to see me come to his rescue.

The enemy thought he was going to destroy not one but

two lives that day. However, my God is a protector and a waymaker who makes a way out of no way. The Lord reminded me, *"The Lord is my rock, my fortress, and my savior; my God is my rock, in whom I find protection. He is my shield, the power that saves me, and my place of safety. (Psalms 18:2, NLT)*

Shortly after that incident, my brother got out of that lifestyle. Today, he is a successful business owner, and I am so proud and grateful for him.

From Family To Single Mother

In 1991, I became pregnant with my first child. I was nervous, happy, excited, and anxious to figure out what was next for me in life. I was unmarried and only had two years working on the force under my belt. The shame I felt was REAL. I knew this was not the way God had intended for me to start a family.

My family was supportive of me; however, my father wasn't happy to hear I was making him a grandfather. After all, I was his baby girl, and he would have preferred me to be married when I had a child. Nonetheless, he stood by me.

"What now, Lord?" I cried. "I know children are a blessing from You, but I'm not ready for a child yet."

God responded through His Word: *"Behold, children are a heritage and gift from the Lord, The fruit of the womb a reward." (Psalm 127:3, AMP)*

While growing up, I cared for my nieces and nephews during the summer months while my sisters worked. I was familiar with the responsibilities of caring for children to some degree, but I wasn't ready to tackle the responsibility of parenting. I thought I was living my best life as an adult because I had a promising career and took care of myself...but I still lived at home.

In 1992, I gave birth to my beautiful baby girl, Denise, whom I absolutely adore. During her early years, I wondered who would care for her while I worked the crazy hours of my job. Many of my family and friends were happy about me becoming a mother, but I struggled to deal with the drastic turn my life had taken. Although being a mother blew my mind, I knew God would be with me every step of the way.

My cousin, Magda, cared for my daughter from the time she was an infant to a toddler while I worked. Words cannot express the love and appreciation I have that she was there for me during that time in my life. I did not want Denise in daycare at such a young age. So, her assistance lifted a heavy burden off of me. Between the pressures of my demanding job and being a single mother, I began questioning my career choice. Was that how I wanted to raise my child—always being at work?

I trusted God to guide me, which wasn't easy. There was so much going on in the city and within the police department, but I hung in there. Unfortunately, my tenacity meant sacrificing my church time; I started attending less and less. Between my extreme workload, raising a small child, and managing a relationship, something had to be sacrificed. I may have limited my time in His house, but a thought came to my mind that God is bigger than my problems and situation.

I took my boyfriend at the time to God in prayer, asking Him if he was the man who He had for me to marry. After all, we already had a child together, which was out of order. When God didn't answer, I asked myself what His silence meant.

As another year went by, the topic of marriage came back around. After setting up counseling sessions, I went before God again in search of direction. God answered this time, telling me the man I was set to marry was not my husband. However, since I believed I could make it work, I did not share with anyone what God had spoken to me. When we think we know more than God, we are operating in our flesh and own understanding—entirely out of His will. Yet, I did my own thing and continued with planning the wedding anyway.

Despite my knowing it was wrong, we proceeded with marriage counseling and were united in holy matrimony in June of 1994. Shortly after, we began attending Mt. Sinai Baptist Church, his family church at the time. Everything went well during the early days of our marriage; however, as time went by, my job and his work schedule became a problem. The fact that God had told me this was not my husband in the first place burned in the back of my mind. We all make mistakes, but a bigger mistake is thinking we have to bear them alone because of the shame.

God will not allow us to believe that having our own understanding or doing things our way will end well without Him. His Word says in *Proverbs 3:5-6 (CSB),*

Irene Reyes-Smith

"Trust in the Lord with all your heart, and do not rely on your own understanding; in all your ways know him, and he will make your paths straight."

Something wasn't right — we were raising a child but neglecting our marriage. At any rate, we did the best we could to make things work. It wasn't long before the days passing by turned into years; it was only God's grace and mercy that kept us.

Eventually, I got pregnant again with my second child, which threw me for a loop. Things were not the way I wanted them to be, especially in my broken marriage. My life turned upside down, and the walls seemed to be crumbling around me. At that point, there was nothing left for me to do but go to God and ask Him why this was happening to me.

"See that you do not despise or think less of one of these little ones, for I say to you that their angels in heaven [are in the presence of and] continually look upon the face of My Father who is in heaven." (Matthew 18:10, AMP)

That was my answer!

In July of 1995, I gave birth to a happy, healthy baby boy we called Junior. Both my kids have the same birthday in July but were born three years apart. What are the chances of that?

"Lord, what are You doing?" I asked.

The Lord replied, *"Every good gift and every perfect gift is from above, and cometh down from the Father of lights, with whom is no variableness, neither shadow of turning." (James 1:17, KJV)*

In 1996, I was still trying to make things work at home so that my kids could have a normal life. Feeling overwhelmed, I brought my concerns to my mother, who advised me to pray and trust God. Although I took her advice, I continued living like I wasn't in church. Still young, I found myself wanting to go out with friends, party, travel, and just do me. I knew how God wanted me to live, and while I had one foot in the church and one foot out of the church, I knew this was not good in the Lord's eyes. I soon realized my young kids needed a lot more of my attention.

The following year, I enrolled Denise and Junior in Calvary Christian Academy, one of the best Christian schools in our area. Giving my children the best Christian foundation was a must. I believed as long as I continued praying, attending church, and raising my kids well, life would get better. In the meantime, I left Mt. Sinai because the connection wasn't there for me anymore. I had been attending out of formality. My soul was empty, and I craved a deeper relationship with God, which was missing.

By age twenty-eight, I started going to Greater Mt. Calvary Holy Church after some urging from my best friend, Nicole. A year and several months went by, and despite attending church, I refused to surrender myself totally to the Lord — even after being prophesied to as an adolescent that God had destined me for greatness. Being part of the church my entire life, I knew in my spirit that God had His hands on me, but my flesh wanted to be more in control. Still, I had to be a mother to my kids.

Irene Reyes-Smith

One evening while reflecting on my life, I heard God say, *"What would it profit you to gain this world and popularity and lose your connection with me?"*

After a while, I found myself in a rut — depressed, stressed, and unsure where or who to turn to. I realized God was isolating me so I would just lay in His presence. The fact that I had not joined Greater Mt. Calvary didn't stop me from meeting with the presiding Bishop A. Owens about my situation. I thanked the bishop for his time, patience, love, and hearing me out, even though I wasn't a member. Rather than dismiss me, he chose to pour into me. I explained that my husband was gone, leaving me to raise our children on my own. The bishop never once passed judgment or looked down on me.

"This too shall pass," he told me. "You aren't the first woman whose husband left and surely not the last. God will work it out. By the way, did the two of you go to marriage counseling?"

"Yes, we did," I confirmed. However, I omitted what God had spoken to me about not marrying my husband.

"I don't know your husband," Bishop Owens replied. "But if he doesn't want to be married anymore, then you know what you have to do."

After our talk, I left the church with tears running down my face and a huge burden lifted off my shoulders. The bishop's words were confirmation of what God already spoke to me earlier that week during my prayer time: *"I will never leave you nor forsake you. Don't be intimidated. Don't worry." (Deuteronomy 31:8, MSG)*

I persevered!

God makes no mistakes. If I may be transparent, I was wearing a mask, wanting people to think my life was all together when it wasn't. God is no respecter of person, but He will keep you in perfect peace if you want to be kept. He will give you a way of escape, as well. Knowing this, I resumed my daily routine while making changes in my life for the better.

At that time, my work schedule was grueling, but thankfully, I received some much-needed help from my family. By the middle of 1997, I had sunken to a place of no return, or so I believed. The church was hosting a revival, and Bishop T.D. Jakes was the special guest who would be preaching. Because I believed attending that service would be the starting point of my genuine relationship with the Lord, I decided to go. Before service was over, God spoke to me. During the altar call, it felt like someone had picked me up from my seat and pushed me to the front to receive Jesus. That's when I truly gave my life over to Him.

Having been in church my entire life, I was well-versed in how to play church without fully surrendering to God as He wants us to. The revival returned me as a babe unto Him, and I was so eager to be in His presence all the time. I believed nothing could stop me!

Renewing my relationship with God made me think everything would be good from then on, but I failed to realize that the devil hears us, too. Seeing I was on a new journey in Christianity, the enemy wanted to take me out mentally and physically, but God had other plans. With little ones to raise, I couldn't be in church all the time as I desired; I had to be there for my kids, as well. I prayed for a solution, and God told me, **"No weapon formed against you shall prosper, and every tongue that rises against you shall be condemned."**

In January of 1998, I joined Greater Mount Calvary Holy Church, a Bible-based, believing church. At first, I couldn't contain the excitement of my new life. However, things took a sudden turn, starting with my separation from my husband. I purchased my first home and was excited about becoming a homeowner but nervous at the same time. My estranged husband didn't make anything easy for me. He refused to be understanding of my work schedule, and there the fight began. I was forced to take the midnight shift, and my parents watched my children while I worked, which was a lot on them.

One night as I crumpled onto the floor in a ball of tears, God said, *"I didn't bring you this far to leave you."* *(Philippians 1:6)* I also remembered Him saying in His Word, **"Weeping may endure for a night, but joy comes in the morning."** After a nudge from the Lord, I surrounded myself with positive and uplifting people who had my best interest at heart. Nevertheless, this scripture came to mind, as well: *"You shall increase my greatness, and comfort me on every side. (Psalm 71:21, NKJV)*

Once the court proceedings for my divorce began, it was an uphill battle that seemed to go on forever. I didn't realize how ill-prepared I was for the ugly, bad, and indifferent I would be slammed with during the proceedings. But I told myself all things are possible with God, and the journey would bring **deliverance, dignity, and humility.**

In June of 1999, my children's father went to their school to pick them up but could only get Junior because Denise wasn't in class at the time. The school wasn't aware of all that had taken place between us. As nightfall approached, my estranged husband had not called to tell me his or Junior's whereabouts. I called his phone incessantly, and he finally picked up.

"When are you bringing Junior home?" I asked hysterically.

In an evil voice, my husband replied, "I'm not."

"Are you serious? What do you mean?"

"I'm keeping Junior. You have one, and now I have one, too."

My mouth dropped to the floor, and my mind began spinning, imagining all sorts of horrific things. Often, we hear of these tumultuous conflicts happening between couples, but it never made sense to me, especially with me being a police officer. Without reaching an amicable resolution, my ex hung up on me. The entire night, I repeatedly called his phone, and we argued until he stopped picking up. The next day when I told my family what had transpired, they were shocked.

I couldn't get my mind off my baby boy and worried about my daughter. What would this do to her? When I dropped her off at school the following day, I advised the staff that if her father attempted to get her, she was not to be released to him. Then I went to the courthouse to file for

Irene Reyes-Smith

an emergency custody order. Unfortunately, I discovered that no parent has the right to a child until custody is established. Therefore, there was nothing I could do except request a court date.

Four months passed before our court date arrived, During that whole time, I had not seen my baby boy. Every day, I wondered what Junior was doing, who he was around, and all sorts of other things. No mother should have to go through what I did. Distraught, I called my friends Lisa and Tiffany for help. On two separate occasions, we went to my estranged husband's job and followed him after his shift to see where he was holding my son. I believe he sensed he was being followed, because we ended up losing him.

Finally, in November, we went to court. The judge ordered that our four-year-old son would stay with his father, while our seven-year-old daughter remained with me. I was devastated! How were things going to get better? How would the hurting stop? When would the pain go away? I slowly began to despise my husband. In my heart, I knew to have hatred toward someone was not Christianlike, but I didn't care. God has a way of humbling us in the most challenging times and reminding us that the battle belongs to Him, but I would have the victory in the end!

I was granted visitation with Junior every weekend; Denise stayed with her father on the fourth weekend. Like clockwork, whenever it was time for my son to go back with his father, he would cry. That was the hardest part for me. I was heartbroken and clueless about how to handle the situation. Taking solace in the fact all of this would be over soon, I comforted my son, assuring him that he would be living with me once again.

The visitations were going well enough until Denise got used to it being just her and me. Her comfort with her brother's absence was disappointing — as I wanted them to be raised together, not apart. As our circumstances worsened and started to become noticeable, my family, friends, church members, and coworkers asked me what was going on and why the judge granted that motion. With no answer to provide, I was left speechless. I could not understand why my ex would want to put the children and me through this. The only thing I could think was that he was trying to make my life miserable and not have to pay support. That's when scripture *II Corinthians 1:13-14 (NKJV)* came to mind: *"Watch, stand fast in the faith, be brave, be strong. Let all that you do be done with love."*

Once again, I needed God to change my attitude towards my ex.

As the kids grew older, their sibling rivalry began. Because they were separated, they believed one was loved more than the other. "Even though we're not living together as a family, I love you both the same, and that will never change," I explained to them. However, Junior started exhibiting excessive anger and behavior issues.

While living with his father, Junior was transferred between three different schools because of his behavior. That was a lot for any child to endure. As I prepared for our next court date, I met with my family and asked for their assistance with Junior in the event the judge granted me custody. I kept the faith that although the road ahead was long, the reward would be great in the end.

In 2001, we went back to court, and to my relief, the judge granted me the divorce and sole custody of both kids; their father received visitation. After hearing the judge's decision, I shouted, "Thank you, Jesus," as tears rolled down my face. I only wish I had known this victory did not mean my ordeal was over.

Because they were the victims of our broken family, I found myself overcompensating with my children to make them feel better. I bought them things, took them out of town, and did whatever else I could to fill the void they were feeling. Spoiling them made things worse, though. Material things couldn't wash away the bitter taste the divorce left on them.

At six years old, I re-enrolled Junior in Calvary Christian Academy with his sister. The move turned out to be extremely good for him because the Christian environment significantly impacted his life. He found comfort in his teachers Ms. Miller and Mrs. Trina, who were like guardian angels sent to guide him when he became overwhelmed and frustrated. He attended the academy from 2002-2005. However, when his behavior spiraled out of control, the school realized he had underlying issues that needed to be addressed in a more intimate, one-on-one setting. As parents, we know our children, but sometimes we are in denial or do not want to accept the truth concerning them.

By the end of the school year, I was on the hunt for another school for him.

The kids' visitation with their father only lasted a month. At one point, I received a call from the school advising me that he had not picked them up. When I called to confront him about it, he let me know he didn't have any intentions of getting them.

"You took me through all of these court proceedings, wasting all this time and money, and now you don't want to spend time with them?" I fussed. "It's all good. We'll be fine. Enjoy your life."

Confused, upset, and frustrated, I sought understanding from the Lord when I felt I couldn't tolerate the situation anymore.

My family told me to go back to court to report my ex-husband was not following orders, but I refused. There was no way the court would make him do anything.

Things ended up getting more chaotic and out of control. Junior was disrespectful at family gatherings, and my brothers would ask what I was going to do about him. My answer to them was that I needed help. Being caught in the middle of a battle between two parents had left him confused and angry.

"Why isn't Dad picking us up anymore? What's going on?" Junior asked out of the blue when he was eight.

The one thing I didn't do was bash my kids' father; I let them develop their own thoughts about him. I didn't have a good answer for my son. So, I skirted the issue and went on with my life as I was accustomed to doing.

Irene Reyes-Smith

My family and friends recommended I get Junior counseling, which frustrated me because they were the same ones who hounded me to get him back from my ex so he could grow up with his sister. Now, they rarely wanted to be bothered with helping me out with him and had an opinion on the situation. Of course, my child was my responsibility, but it takes a village to raise a child, right?

I ended up enrolling Junior in activities and camps to provide him with outlets to express himself, but I received phone calls requesting me to pick him up because he was misbehaving. At the onset, I stayed strong, but alone in my room at night, I would break down in tears.

The church had a program called Son's Ministry for single moms raising young boys. So, I enrolled Junior. He struggled at first, not being able to do what he wanted to do with the Christian men in the church. The program was structured, and Junior looked up to several mentors: Eric, Mr. Steve, Mr. Grant, Mr. Thornton, and Pastor Will — all of whom had an immense impact on his life. He stuck with the program for three years, mainly because he could not get out of it as easily as the other programs he had been involved in. The program did him some good for the moment.

As things continued to deteriorate, I was faced with deciding between my children and my job, and in no way was it easy. Of course, as a mother, you do what's necessary to take care of your kids. I talked it over with family members and then prayed. Desperate and without waiting for a definitive answer from God, I let my emotions guide me and decided to quit my job as a police officer, opting to accept a position as a project manager for a company with comparable pay to what I was making. I truly believed this was the best move, but unfortunately, the job didn't work out as I expected.

Once that job fell through, I found myself back at the police department, this time assigned to the Fourth District station, working the streets of D.C., and right back to a hectic schedule. *There has to be something else I can do,* I told myself, then prayed about it. Little did I know our community outreach coordinator was looking for someone to assist her with community events in the summer — exactly what I enjoyed doing! The opportunity would allow me to assist single mothers with their male children by recommending and implementing programs, mentors, and prayer — everything I knew to do. I asked God to help me be the pillar of light who would shine to let others know He is with them. I spent the rest of that year as Community Outreach Officer, in charge of community outreach programs.

In August of 2005, I registered Junior in LaSalle Middle School, where he attended for a year. Once again, his attitude and behavior weren't conducive to the school's environment, and they advised me to get Junior tested for issues with structure, authority, ADHD, and emotional behavior. As his mother, I immediately went on defensive mode, refusing to have my child labeled or put on medication. I began praying and asking God to show me what my next course of action should be regarding Junior. It wasn't easy, but it was worth it.

"Lord, I thank You because things could have turned out another way," I told God one day. I kept giving thanks and adoring Jesus because I had considered doing the unthinkable after all I had been through with my ex-husband. Life had gotten the best of me, and some days I felt helpless. But God recognized the strength that I failed to see in myself because of all my hurt, pain, pride, frustration, guilt, and shame.

I reminded myself that I am the daughter of the Most High, and there's nothing too hard for God. Drastic measures had to be taken to get things back on track, so I swallowed my pride and called my ex-husband.

"I'm only going to say this once; until you do right by your kids, your life will never be the same," I warned him.

Life and death are in the power of the tongue, but he needed to hear that. I had to be the bigger person for God to release me from the hurt, frustration, and anger that was consuming me. I gave it all to God — my ex-husband, my issues, my circumstances — and forgave him. It was time to move on.

That summer, along with some of my co-workers, I started working at MPDC summer camps for inner-city youth who were not old enough to work. The program was a success, and I developed wonderful relationships with many of the kids. I took Junior with me to camp so he could see how fortunate he was and how other kids his age were appreciative of the little things in life. Sadly, his behavior didn't change much. One of the other officers working at the camp noticed how I was struggling with Junior and asked if I wanted their friend, who was good with young males, to speak with him. I agreed, and following their conversation, Junior's behavior subsided.

I met Officer K. Parker while working with the MPDC summer camps. He asked if I would be interested in working with him in truancy because he needed a female partner. After understanding what the position entailed, I accepted the offer, thinking it would be a great experience. Being bilingual was a plus, and given what I was going through with Junior, I welcomed the opportunity to help other children. God has a way of using our situation to help others.

At the end of my rope with my wayward son, I spoke with my niece, Janet. She always maintained a positive outlook and prayed on my behalf. Junior was ten, and I needed to do something to straighten him out before he started heading the wrong way. We researched options on the internet and discovered Reality Ranch Military Camp. It was expensive, but I was willing to make the sacrifice to save Junior's life.

Since the camp only lasted a few weeks in the summer, I still needed to figure something out for the upcoming school year. So, I registered Junior in Francis Stevens Middle School for the 2005-2006 school year. Yet again, the school determined Junior's attitude and behavior were inappropriate, and for a second time, I was advised to have him tested for issues with structure, authority, ADHD, and

Irene Reyes-Smith

emotional misbehavior.

That summer, several other officers and I came up with a plan to help keep the youth off the streets. We named our idea *Playstreets*. We shut the streets down in various neighborhoods throughout the Fourth District, cooked on the grill, opened the hydrants, and had activities allowing us to interact with the kids. It was a safe, fun, positive environment that lasted the entire summer and fostered positive relationships between us, the kids, and the community. Our mission was to establish long-lasting relationships and boost the community's confidence that we were there to serve them. Due to overwhelming success, *Playstreets* became an annual event every summer!

Despite the success of my community involvement, with Junior getting older and more unmanageable, I was left with difficult decisions to make for the upcoming school year. One would think that as an officer, I would have all the resources and help I needed at my disposal, but I did not. As a result, I was embarrassed, and my pride took a hit.

While wallowing in my pain, I heard the Lord telling me that I wasn't alone. Still too embarrassed to reach out for the help I desperately needed, I remained silent. Police officers find it hard to ask for assistance because we're the ones who are supposed to offer help, especially when it comes to our children. I spoke to several officer friends who assured me everything would be alright, but I had to be honest with myself. I let my family, close friends, and church family know about the restless nights, hurt, fear, embarrassment, and sacrifices I was dealing with and how I constantly cried myself to sleep because I dreaded the next day. It was time to be transparent.

The school year started rough. I was working as a truant officer and loved my position. Being able to help inner-city youth get to school on time and further their education was a dream. My work schedule and hours were good, which afforded me the time to get better control of my kids' life and education. However, Junior didn't want to get up for school. That's when I would have my neighbors or brothers go to the house to get him up.

My schedule required me to be in the office before school started for the day, which sometimes worked, but most often, it didn't. Why? Because I would have to go back home to get Junior and take him to school. Thanks to my partner at the time – Kenneth – for being in my corner when I needed it most. I was at my wit's end and crying in the truancy van while venting and agonizing over my son. Kenneth encouraged me, reminding me that I am a God-fearing woman who knows how to pray.

I didn't understand why I had to experience what I was going through but felt it was bigger than me, so I pressed on.

"Draw near to God, and he will draw near to you."
(James 4:8, ESV)

No matter what I did to help, protect, and isolate my child, it seemed nothing worked. The enemy had me believing he wanted my son. One Sunday evening after church service ended, I spoke to a minister who told me about a Christian boarding school in Indiana. I wasn't certain if that's what I wanted for Junior or how I would even pay for it. Yet, God provided every step of the way.

The following school year, Junior was seriously smelling himself at eleven years old. It was time to take drastic measures. I told myself that I had to do something before he got into more serious trouble. In the meantime, I worked hard at letting Junior know there was nothing in the streets. I stressed to him that I only wanted the best for him. When he found out my plan to send him away to school, he promised to behave if I let him stay with me. Being as persuasive as he was, I consented. However, his good behavior only lasted briefly, so off he went to Indiana.

My nephew Jaime accompanied me to take Junior to school. By the grace of God, he was admitted since he wasn't twelve years of age as the school required. Because a minister from my church had recommended us to the school, they took him. When I asked God if I was doing the right thing, or if I would regret sending Junior away, this scripture flooded my spirit: ***"God comforts and strengthens us in our hardships and trials. God will give you strength to endure." (II Corinthians 1:13-14)***

After I completed all the necessary paperwork, Junior was all set. Before we left, Jaime chatted with him, explaining that he needed to show me that he could behave, listen, and be respectful while he was there. Then maybe he would be allowed to return home.

"Your mom loves you," Jamie told him.

"'No, she doesn't!" Junior yelled. "If she did, she

wouldn't be shipping me away!"

I rushed to my own defense, hoping to change the way Junior felt.

"I do love you, man! I want the best for you, but you're just not listening, and I don't want to lose you to the streets."

My words didn't help, though. Junior viewed my actions as otherwise.

The registrar assured me that Junior would be fine, and we left the office for a campus tour. The school had a vigorous and strict schedule, which I liked, but Junior didn't. As the tour came to an end, Junior grabbed my leg and screamed for me not to leave him there. This broke my heart, but I had to do it. When we left the building, he took off running into a nearby field. The chaperone advised me there was nowhere for Junior to go, and they would handle it.

A month went by, and Junior sent letters begging to come home to be with his sister and me. In response, I asked how school was and how he was doing. At first, he answered back negatively. He constantly earned bad marks on his progress reports. However, as time went on, the reports became positive. Junior was adapting, and his teachers sent good progress notes. My heart was filled with joy!

I prayed Junior would be safe since he was at a vulnerable age and the youngest at the school. When he called us on the phone, Denise kept the conversation short. I asked if she wanted to speak to her brother longer, but she complained that I catered to Junior and gave him special treatment ever since he lived with my ex-husband. I denied it and tried to convince her that he was going through a little more than her and needed extra help. I let her know I loved them equally and would do anything to keep them safe. When the school hosted events and family days, Denise drove with me and a few other relatives and me to Indiana to spend time with Junior. I went as often as I could to show my love and support.

After a year, Junior asked me when he was coming home. He was adamant that he had been doing what he was supposed to and was on his good behavior. The thing is, Junior had a way of convincing people that he had changed when he really hadn't. He even asked who would protect Denise and me with him away at school, which made me chuckle. He believed he was indeed the man of our house. Though I didn't agree to bring him home, the Lord told me, *"The devil wants your son, but I created him for greatness."*

I burst into tears because God's declaration over Junior transported me back to when I was a child. I remember having nightmares of someone chasing me around a burning bush trying to kill me. When I told my mother, she said to keep praying because the enemy was after me, but God had me. I immediately prayed, calling out Junior's name, and told Satan, "You won't have any child of mine!" Using prayer as my weapon, I did the best I could as a mother to keep Junior safe.

At the end of the school year, Junior returned home with

minimal incidents. I enrolled him in golf and football to keep him occupied, but by mid-summer, he quit football in favor of golf, which he loved. At summer's end, I had the daunting task of finding a new school to enroll him in.

On July 12th, 2007, my world came crashing down with my mother's sudden death. In a state of disbelief, I cried out, "Why, Lord! Why, Lord! Not my mother!" But it was true. I knew Mom had some health issues, but I didn't believe they were that serious.

Being the two grandkids who spent the most time with my parents, my kids were hysterical. Junior, who had a special bond with my mother, took it the hardest. She prayed over him the most and had him and Denise in church several days a week. That's how I knew for sure God had His hand on their lives. Mom's death took a toll on Junior and led him down a path of destruction, as my mother was always there when he needed her. Mom was the rock of the family.

Following Mom's death, I enrolled Junior in MacFarland Middle School. Although the school had the program he needed, I knew its location wasn't in the best area. Sometimes, I'd be at work nervous, hoping my son went to school that day and wasn't one of the kids hanging outside the school building instead of going to class.

The program Junior was enrolled in required him to leave his regular class for "specials" because of the assistance he needed. He started great because he had a big heart for helping, just like I did. His teacher often reported that Junior assisted the kids with more severe problems and situations and was a role model. He constantly ensured his classmates were alright. Unfortunately, all of Junior's hard work was in vain.

Everything changed when Junior's friends noticed he was leaving class for special assistance. Feeling he didn't need the class, Junior no longer wanted to be part of it. I told him not to worry about what other people thought of him and that if they were truly his friends, what he was doing wouldn't matter to them. Peer pressure is real, though. Guess what? His behavior started getting worse. Bombarded with calls about how he was acting up, I attempted to enlist my brothers, Junior's mentors, and male ministers from the church to check on him at school, visit with his teachers, and attend meetings. He was getting into fights and hanging out with the wrong crowd.

At this time, MPDC enlisted officers to work inside the schools, and from time to time, they called me to drop in the school because Junior was misbehaving again. Later, I discovered he was being bullied and teased by other students. I reminded him that I wasn't just his mother; I was the "PO-PO" (short for police), and he didn't have to misbehave to fit in and be cool. I wanted Junior to understand that when God has a calling on your life, sometimes you are set apart, and God's hand of protection was on him.

The pressure of my profession affected Junior, too. I was picking up his friends for truancy and dropping them off at school. The program wasn't working in his favor, and he was suspended from school on four different occasions.

One of those suspensions resulted in him being arrested for possession of a controlled substance. I rushed to find a good child advocacy representative and program to help him, which happened quickly. He was enrolled in High Roads, an inclusionary school for children in Maryland. He didn't understand why he couldn't just stay where he was, but the move was crucial to saving his life.

High Roads was a big adjustment for Junior, and he experienced major ups and downs. There were days he would miss the bus on purpose, and I'd have to make arrangements to get him to school. Other days, he went late with a bad attitude. I would constantly remind Junior just to make the best of the school and time would go by fast. Junior was not happy with the decision since the school was in Maryland, and there was no easy access for him to the city. I had to remind Junior that the Lord was always there for him during these confusing times in his adolescent years. The scripture *Isaiah 58:9* came to mind: *"Then you will call, and the Lord will answer; you will cry for help, and he will say: Here am I."*

"I am with you always, even until the end of the world," God told me. When I asked for confirmation that it was truly Him, *Psalms 46:1* dropped in my spirit: *"God is our refuge and strength, a very present help in time of trouble."* I already knew by the end of the school year that I would have to find yet another school for Junior because my family and friends weren't going to keep going to the house to take him to school. A friend referred me to New Beginnings Vocational School, which I believed would

work out great for us.

Again, Junior started off great—getting up on time and attending school regularly. There was a different structure. The staff was wonderful; the kids worked at their own pace and were assigned trades to learn, which Junior loved. He took up automotive and woodshop. There was a spark in him that I hadn't seen before. He had finally found his niche and loved the experience he was getting. He also met a young man who steered him in the right direction, and they became the best of friends. Won't God do it?

I believed the worst was over, until one day, Junior dropped the bomb that he was introduced to various drugs while he was away at boarding school. I was furious.

Unfazed by my shock, Junior said, "See, Ma, you sent me away to a boarding school to help me, and look what I learned there."

I couldn't believe it. The embarrassment I felt for delivering my son into the hands of drugs kept me from ever telling anyone what he had confided in me. I never called the school to ask if they knew about the drug activity. Instead, I asked Junior if he had tried any of them for himself. He said he hadn't, but the boys taught him how to start selling and making a lot of money. The enemy thought he would control Junior's life with fast money and drugs.

The devil is a liar, I told myself.

I had many of my mother's ways and remembered how she taught us that money doesn't grow on trees. She also taught us how to save and not overspend, which my children loved to do. It was easy to see why Junior was tempted by that lifestyle. The ways of this world are wicked and will have us believe that the finer things in life matter the most. But I believe material things aren't what makes us. Our beliefs, morals, life encounters, and God's word is what keeps us.

God Was My Guide

The Bible is a book of prayers, guides, examples, and teachings that we are supposed to live by. I didn't know back then my authority on the job came from the Lord, as ordained from the beginning with the soldiers in His army. The same way Christ can change our lives, I needed to recognize the power of being able to change the lives of others. Nothing is by happenstance, but by every miracle and action of God.

When my life was in shambles, *Psalms 34:19, AMP* carried me through: *"Many hardships and perplexing circumstances confront the righteous, but the Lord rescues him from them all."* I thank God for the **process** to secure my **promise.**

The same equipment God provided for me on the job in the secular world is the equipment I use in the spiritual realm:

- *The Helmet of Salvation = God kept my mind on Him.*
- *The Breastplate of Righteous = My vest.*
- *The Belt of Truth = My belt with my equipment on it.*
- *The Sword of the Spirit/God's Word = The law of the land.*
- *The Shield of Faith = My shield, God's protection.*
- *Gospel Shoes = My boots and the direction of God.*

My trials were ordained for God to get the Glory, and man would see it was Him who brought me out. No weapon, condemnation, or judgment came upon me.

When The Badge Comes Home

Years 2010-2013 were intense, indescribable, and fearful. Junior was struggling to figure out his next move. He was attending vocational school, but instead of doing what he needed to do to graduate successfully, he started missing classes again.

"What's going on with you?" I asked him. "I know the last couple of years have been rough, and you're dealing with a lot, but I need you to focus so you can graduate."

Junior shrugged off my concern, and a part of me felt like I was losing him.

Several nights a week, I rode through the neighborhoods where I believed Junior was hanging out—searching the streets, praying, crying, and calling his phone simultaneously. Dealing with him was so stressful. It seemed like the more I did to help my son, the more intense things became. I slowly realized this was the start of something I wasn't ready to face. I also began to notice that my focusing on Junior more was drawing a wedge between him and his sister, which had me praying even more for her, as well.

One day, my mother spoke to me regarding my son. She referred to me as *Bing*, her term of endearment for me.

"Bing, you have to continue to pray. Be specific with the prayer and truly give Junior to God, as only He knows best," I heard her tell me as tears rolled down my face.

Mom was gone, but her voice still provided me with guidance and direction. Dad was older and didn't know much about the younger generation, and my brothers had done all they were going to do but were around if I needed them. My coworkers, church family, and neighbors assisted, as well, but the only real solution I had was God Himself. I had to truly *LET GO* and *LET GOD* for my son to see the manifestation of God working in His life.

Despite having a village to support me, on those nights when Junior wouldn't come home by his curfew time, I was too ashamed to call anyone for help. Instead, I would call his phone, and he would claim he was on his way home but failed to show up. No one knew the pain and hurt I was enduring from this child.

This behavior went on for some time until one day, I sat Junior down and told him, "I can't keep this up. I'm tired of your disrespect, your behavior, and your attitude. It's getting old! I'm trying to work my job, and chasing behind you has exhausted me. You have to change right now. Otherwise, this isn't going to end well. I'm going to end up burying you, or you'll be in jail."

"Don't talk like that, Ma," Junior simply responded, leaving me with nothing more to do or say.

Prayer and God's promise to me over Junior's life were the only things keeping me going.

In the summer of 2010, one of Junior's friends was tragically killed while celebrating at one of the events during Georgia Avenue Day. Junior was there, as well. He said when the gunshots rang out, all of his friends ran. He ran past his friend, and by the time he reached the end of the block, he was no longer there. Junior doubled back and discovered his friend had been struck by a bullet and was dead. Junior called me crying profusely over the phone.

The tragedy took a toll on Junior, and he wasn't the same after that day. He laid low, staying with family members and friends because I wasn't allowing him to bounce in and out of my house. I tried explaining that his way of living wasn't good, and I wanted more for him. I told him that God had His hands on him, but Junior couldn't see his future the way I could. Only God could intervene on his behalf, but I had to get out of God's way! It was hard for me but required!

My life was stressful and chaotic, but God knew what was best for Junior. I needed help and wanted to be married again, but I didn't believe the time was right. My son's out-of-control behavior was a stark contrast to my line of work, and if it was God's will for me to be married again, I believed He would send a God-fearing man who loved me as he loved the church. If not, being a single mother would have to do.

Amid the turmoil in my life, I met a man I didn't feel was "the one." Although his personality and conversation were good, I wasn't going to allow my FLESH to take control again. When he expressed he was attracted to my spirit and my walk with the Lord, it piqued my interest. After several months of dating, I asked God to send a sign if he was the one. I didn't get it right away, but I did get my sign: All was well.

God operates on His timing, not ours. What we want may not come when we think it should, but He is always on time!

"When am I going to meet your kids?" he casually asked one day.

"Soon," I replied, all the while thinking about the destructive path Junior was on and how his behavior might affect my new relationship.

Junior refused to listen to me and wanted to be his own authoritarian. I figured the two of them would clash. How would he deal with Junior? What would he think about my parenting methods? How would Junior react towards him?

After a couple of weeks passed, I decided to introduce him to the kids. I didn't need any more complications in my life, but I figured there would never be a perfect time for this. From what I could tell when they met, the kids seemed to be alright with him. Junior didn't seem to be too interested, and if I was happy, so was Denise. A few weeks later, I asked what he thought about my kids after meeting them.

"They'll come around," he told me.

As I got more comfortable being with him, my children

began to see more of him, as well.

One evening when I asked Junior to take out the trash, he snapped, "Have your friend do it." There was a bit of back and forth between us, but he did it. My boyfriend was shocked. More and more, he witnessed Junior's disrespectful behavior towards me.

"I don't know what your son has been through," he said, "but I can't tolerate disrespect."

Shortly after, they bumped heads, and the verbal disagreements between them began. My boyfriend couldn't stand seeing Junior act the way he did towards me, especially with all I had done for him as a single mother. If we were going to stay together, he didn't want to be silent about what he saw. When I recounted everything that happened with Junior before he came into my life, my boyfriend replied, "That's still no excuse for him to treat you like that! Given the circumstances, you've done the best you can."

Months passed by, and Facetiming with my boyfriend dwindled to just talking on the phone. Wanting to save my relationship, I sat Junior down and told him that I liked my boyfriend and wanted to be married again. He didn't want to hear it, but it was reality. By now, he was hanging out more, smoking, and involved in illegal activities I didn't even know about. Things had ramped up to another level.

My life was in shambles. It was now the middle of June in 2011. My daughter was having a baby, I was in a new relationship, and Junior was even more out of control. I just wanted to crawl under a rock. I could not believe everything that was happening to me—a God-fearing woman who believed in all God had promised me and walking in my purpose.

On September 28, 2011, the Lord woke me early in the morning and instructed me to go into my son's room and anoint his head, room, shoes, and bed. Obediently, I did. Later that evening, I had Denise drive to my aunt's house to get Junior, but he didn't want to come home.

I called him and said, "Junior, come home now. You know when I have to call you two or three times, something always happens."

Of course, he ignored me. Hours later, I received a call from Washington Hospital Center notifying me that Junior had been shot. My heart dropped, and immediately, I began crying and praying.

When I arrived at the hospital, the police and detectives were already there, but they would not tell me anything. They took me to the back where detectives were questioning Junior. Since he refused to respond, they asked me to speak to him to get the details of what happened. However, my only concern at the time was ensuring my son was alright.

"Had I not been obedient to the Holy Spirit, you wouldn't be here right now," I fussed.

"Really, Mom?"

"Yes!"

Junior turned to look at me with sincerity in his eyes. "I know, Ma. I love you."

In my head, I said, *Thank you, Jesus. I know what you*

promised me!

I told him I loved him, too, but that he had to change.

Finally, he recounted the night's events.

Junior and his friends saw a car approaching them. The young men inside the car jumped out and started shooting, and Junior and his friends ran to escape death. I had him repeat the story to the detectives, who believed there was more than what Junior shared. Although the other boys were severely injured and one of them was left paralyzed, Junior's injuries were minor. He was shot in the thumb, and a bullet grazed the top of his foot…in the very shoes I had anointed that morning.

When we got home from the hospital, I told Junior, "You see, God sends signs. We have to be still and walk in obedience with Him to hear them. You are a covered man from your grandmother's prayers and mine. I just need you to listen."

"I am, Mom," he assured me, and he did well for a while.

Needing support and male insight, I spent more time with my male friend, who, of course, said I needed to get a handle on things with Junior before things got further out of control.

I wasn't sure whether my friend intended to stay in my life or leave. It seemed like I was crazy for even wanting to bring a man into such chaos, but God said, *"For I know the plans I have for you," declares the Lord, "plans to prosper you and not to harm you, plans to give you hope and a future." (Jeremiah 29:11, NIV)* Only God has the answers and makes sense out of the foolishness in our lives.

Irene Reyes-Smith

The questions were coming regarding the shooting Junior had been involved in. However, I never received a call or any correspondence about the incident. Little did I know my son was on the investigator's radar.

"Lord, I need Your help now more than ever before," I pleaded.

My career was what it was, and my God protected it.

In the middle of 2011, still apprehensive about things between my new man and me, I prayed for understanding, wisdom, endurance, and the strength to raise Junior in a happy, stress-free environment. Even after escaping death, Junior started showing off more than before—staying out all night doing who knows what with who knows who. I demanded he stop, warning that street life was going to catch up with him. He refused to hear me, though. Still, I reminded him that God is gracious and merciful but wanted Junior to be obedient. Then I provided him with this scripture: *"Honor your mother and father, that your days may be long upon the land which the Lord your God is giving you." (Exodus 20:12, NKJV)*

Despite all my urging for him to change his life, my advice fell on deaf ears. Junior continued getting in trouble and was arrested on several occasions for illegal drug substance and minor infractions.

"Do you ever think about the job that I do?" I asked him. When he confirmed he did, I said, "Then why do you keep on with the foolishness you're doing and embarrassing me? These are my co-workers! This is my career!"

I explained several officers told me that they had seen

Junior hanging around known felons and trying to fit in, and they offered to talk to him. I was humiliated. Some of the officers talked behind my back, questioning how I could allow Junior to behave this way, but God reassured me there is no perfect child nor parent. My true friends stood by me and uplifted me, telling me God had His hand upon my son. I can remember being in the locker room at work crying sometimes. In life, we tend to point fingers, ridicule, and speak ill of others, but by God's grace, we all have been saved and need to pray for those who aren't there yet. Lord knows I love my son, but he didn't want to listen.

I took my tragedy and turned it into triumph, but the enemy was mad that I was walking by faith in my purpose with the Lord. He couldn't get to me anymore, so he attacked my seed (my son). Spiritually, I started fighting with the Armor of God and His Word. The enemy wasn't giving up that easily, and neither was I. The battle belongs to God, but the victory belongs to me!

Junior turned seventeen and was messing up in school, so I called to request a meeting with the principal who I had a good rapport with. Junior slowly realized his mistakes were catching up to him and was trying to change but failed to see how we all have to take into account our actions, whether good or bad. He apologized for the things he put me through, and I encouraged him to do better. He was wrestling with his purpose from God, coupled with peer pressure and street life. The enemy is a deceiver!

Growing up a male minority is hard, and Junior saw and

experienced so many horrible things as a child. It takes a village to raise kids, but that concept seems to have been thrown out the window with today's society. This generation is missing it. Without his village to hold him accountable, Junior hung with the wrong crowds and did what he wanted to get what he thought were the good things in life. That's when against my wishes, he went back to living with friends.

In spite of the madness, life took a positive turn, and I got engaged. I wasn't sure if my children were on the same page as me, but they were getting older and doing their own thing, and I needed a change, too.

My fiancé and I started marriage counseling. In class, we intently listened to the instructions and material presented, but once class was over, we would get in heated discussions about things that transpired between us, the children, or something said in class. We decided to speak with the instructors to get their perspective on our conflicts, as the blended family between all of our kids was new to us, but we were willing to see it through. The counselors said we needed to decide if marriage was what we both wanted since we came from two different backgrounds and our parenting styles were different. They recommended we get in the Word of God to see what He says about marriage, as we knew we wanted God to be the third strand cord in it.

Later that year, as things progressed with premarital counseling and wedding planning, the enemy got busy. My fiancé and I were relaxing and watching a movie one evening, when Junior came home late, needing something out of my room. When I told him what he was looking for wasn't in there, he insisted it was and began cursing at me. My fiancé became upset and demanded he respect me, but Junior told him to stay out of it. The two exchanged words, and things escalated to the point where I had to intervene. Things went too far, but God allows certain things to take place to expose what needs to be addressed.

Out of guilt for the things he had dealt with in life, I had never spoken forcefully to Junior, and therefore, he made the mistake of thinking he was the man of the house. He believed no man should have been able to enter the home where he grew up and tell him what to do. His attitude was a disaster I created and had to fix, starting with letting him know my fiancé was going to be part of his life, whether he accepted it or not. That night ended painfully.

Disheartened, I cried out to God, "This is the man You sent me, Lord! Now look what's transpiring!"

Then Jesus said, *"Come to me, all of you who are weary and carry heavy burdens, and I will give you rest. Take my yoke upon you. Let me teach you, because I am humble and gentle at heart, and you will find rest for your souls. For my yoke is easy to bear, and the burden I give you is light."* *(Matthew 11:28-30, NLT)*

Without a shadow of a doubt, I knew my fiancé was the one. My faith was unstoppable, and even when the enemy tried to stop me, I stood on God's Word for every area of my life. I wasn't perfect, but I leaned on God's everlasting love.

It seemed like the wedding was off. Had I lost the love of my life? A few days passed without us speaking. He finally called and said we needed to talk, and I was ecstatic to hear from him. When we got together, I tearfully told him I would understand if he wanted to break off our engagement.

"I know people are going to think I'm crazy for wanting to stay with you," he said.

I responded by saying, "We can't allow people to dictate our lives or what God wants for us, not even our children. They're getting older and moving on with their lives."

Serious changes needed to be made between us, especially on my part. We stayed in counseling and became more in tune with God's Word. The enemy continued with his schemes, but we stood together on God's Word, not allowing anything or anyone to intervene. We finished the class and received our certificate of completion, then went on with our wedding plans as scheduled. The date was set for August of 2013. Junior didn't come around much, and Denise didn't make too much of a fuss.

We made it through 2012! My faith kept me—my mind, my "yes," my favor. I was ambitious, energetic, totally committed, and humble.

A few months into 2013, my father's health began to fail. I was heartbroken because Dad was my hero. With Mom gone, he was the one I talked to about my fiancé and was supposed to walk me down the aisle. My brother Tony called me to meet with the doctor concerning Dad's health, and we were told he would be put on home hospice. He was given between a month to a year to live, which didn't sit well with me. Mom was already gone. Why did I have to lose Dad, too? I refused to accept the diagnosis.

I remember the morning of March 14, 2013, like it was yesterday. We were out running some errands, getting things together for our wedding, and had stopped at TGI Friday's for a bite to eat. As we dined, I received a call from the home health aide nurse, reporting my father wasn't breathing right. I told her to call his doctor, and I would be on my way. About an hour later, I received another call that my dad wasn't breathing, and we rushed to get to him. When we pulled up to the house, I swung open the door and raced upstairs to where my father was lying in bed. He was already gone.

"No!" I wailed at the top of my lungs. "No, Papi!"

Sobbing uncontrollably, I wasn't ready for him to go, but I knew he was in a better place.

My brother cleared the room, asking everyone to give me some time alone with Papi. My mind raced; I was a bundle of emotions. My fiancé came back into the room and told me that Papi had given him his blessing to marry me. He told him to take good care of me, and my fiancé assured him he would. Both of my parents were gone. What would my life be like now? Who would I go to about my life issues?

My children were devastated by their grandfather's death. Junior took it especially hard because he and Denise spent a lot of time over my parents' house helping them. A couple of months after Papi's death, I told my fiancé that the wedding was off.

"Are you serious?" he asked.

"Yes, my father is gone, and he was supposed to walk me down the aisle," was my response.

"You're just upset," he reasoned. "I know it hurts, but I promised him I would take care of you."

Broken, I asked for time to gather my feelings before I made a final decision.

I reached out to my brother for advice on what I should do. He told me if I was happy with my fiancé, not to worry about the kids or anything else because they would go off to live their lives, and I would end up alone. He was right; we only get one life, and mine was a purpose-filled one. Later that evening, I went before God in quietness to hear the still small voice of Jesus, and I received my answer! The next day, I called my fiancé, and we talked. By the end of our conversation, the wedding was back on.

The morning of our wedding, I saw Junior and asked if he was coming. Very coolly, he responded no. Hearing my child say he wouldn't be there for my big day hurt me to the core. My sister, Joe, saw my pain and told me not to worry and that Junior would come around. She was only trying to comfort me, but his absence was still hurtful.

After we married, my family was extremely happy for me. My husband is an extraordinary, loving, and amazing man. Life was incredible, and we were in the honeymoon stage.

In December of 2013, while we were on a cruise with family and friends, my husband received a call from my brother-in-law that Junior had been shot again!

Please, God! It can't be true.

My brother-in-law didn't have all the details and said we would call us back. My family tried to calm me down and began praying, which was all we could do. The next call I received was from Junior's father telling me that he was on his way to the hospital. As it turned out, supposedly, it was a drive-by shooting, and Junior had been shot a few inches below his eye. If it weren't for the bone where the bullet was lodged, he would've lost his eye or even his life.

The following week when I returned home and went to see Junior, I read him this scripture: ***"But I need something more! For I know the law but still can't keep it, and if the power of sin within me keeps sabotaging my best intentions, I obviously need help! I realize that I don't have what it takes. I can will it, but I can't do it. I decide to do good, but I don't really do it; I decide not to do bad, but then do it anyway. My decisions, such as they are, don't result in actions. Something has gone wrong deep within me and gets the better of me every time. It happens so regularly that it's predictable. The moment I decide to do good, sin is there to trip me up." (Romans 7:19-21, The MSG)***

"Enough is enough," I admonished Junior. "You have to rise above this and stop. The enemy wants your soul, but God has your mind, and you have to realize you belong to Him. The plans God has for your life will flourish when you surrender to Him. I raised you in church, so you know how to pray and seek God. There's nothing good in these streets. You are eighteen years old and have to do something different with your life if you want different results. I don't even want to know the circumstances behind this last situation. I have to keep myself safe and sane."

The hedge of protection around Junior also shielded me from his chaos and crime.

While I was still adjusting to my new blended family, Denise was a single mother to a four-year-old and needed my help.

Having been there myself and knowing the struggle, my husband and I assisted her as much as we possibly could. No grandchild of mine would grow up in poverty or powerless. I often wondered if I paid too much attention to my son, leaving Denise to feel that she had to take care of herself to a degree. I sometimes felt like I opened the door for the enemy to come in and take some control over my daughter's life because my focus was on Junior so much— the attention and guidance for Denise were somewhat put to the side. As mothers, we are often spread thin, but I felt Denise would be more self-sufficient than Junior because of the way I was raising her. The reality is she still needed my love, direction, and assurance. I believe when we focus on the Word of God more and truly seek Him, He will show us the path and purpose He has for us and even our family. I know life won't be a cakewalk. Trials, tribulations, and tragedies will occur, but while trusting in the Lord, it won't be as burdensome as we may think.

From time to time, I would see Junior and ask him if he

was doing alright or needed anything. Sometimes he said he was fine. Other times he asked for money to eat or buy clothes. In reality, Junior wasn't doing well at all. Following the shooting, he was in pain and had other health conditions. On top of that, he needed therapy. I agreed to make the appointments and go with him if I needed to. Our relationship was in a better place, but I couldn't allow him to live with me anymore. That part of my life was over.

As the year went on, several of Junior's friends were killed or incarcerated. I praised God when he called to say, "Ma, I have to get a job and change my life." After making some calls, my brother agreed to hire Junior, but he had to be on time and do his work. When I gave Junior the good news, I told him that his uncle didn't play when it came to business but was willing to give him a chance. About six months after beginning work, Junior started showing up late and doing a poor job. He didn't understand that it wasn't a game. Business is business, even when you're doing business with family. Consequently, he was fired.

It took getting fired for Junior to realize how good he had it and what having good work ethics meant. He apologized to his uncle and searched for another job. From that experience, he learned that we have to value what we have in life, especially when it comes easily. I know it hurt Junior, but it had to happen.

A Mother's Worst Nightmare

I finally faced the reality that my son wanted to indulge in things that would lead him down the road that had not been ordained for him, but I never stopped praying. It was 2015, and now twenty years old, Junior was still trying to get his life in order. I wasn't surprised when I got word he had been arrested again. I didn't even flinch when he called collect from the jail to apologize for all he had done to embarrass me.

I fussed at him for doing what he wanted despite my advice, but I didn't want to keep harping on that. When he informed me that he was locked up for possession and other charges, I didn't even reply. I hadn't imagined my son being behind bars, so I was at a loss for words. All the love, conversations, nurturing, guidance, stress, pain, and direction I had given him came to a screeching halt. I had to put on my belt of truth!

The system is set up so that young black males who are repeat offenders are sometimes targets, and their activity is monitored until age twenty-one. At twenty-one years old, they are aged out of the juvenile system and become targeted adults. If this cycle isn't broken, the individual is bound to continue the life of criminal activity. I believe it takes a village and a mindset change to turn around the mentality of our youth today.

Junior was assigned a court-appointed lawyer who was excellent and knew her stuff. He had numerous court dates and hearings to get released on house arrest, but each attempt was denied. The in and out of jail had finally caught Junior in his tracks, and I accepted what God allowed.

Seeing Junior locked up when I visited him brought tears to my eyes.

"Ma, please tell everyone I said hello, and that I miss and love them," he would somberly say.

The hardest part was when visiting time was over, and I had to leave. I pondered about all the times I prayed and anointed my child, only for him to end up imprisoned. The thought was excruciating.

"It had to happen like this," God said, *"because he wasn't listening and was going to end up dead."*

It was difficult not being able to call Junior when I wanted to speak to him and enduring the stress of wondering if my co-workers knew my circumstances. Everyone would tell me that at least I knew where Junior was now and could be at peace. I understood where they were coming from, but it didn't ease my pain. At least there were no more late-night rides or wondering if I would get a call saying he was injured or dead. No mother wants to have to experience receiving collect phone calls, having visitations behind glass, or hearing their child's distressed voice on the other end of the phone and not be able to help them physically or mentally. Every time we finished talking, I would break down in tears.

I found some comfort by staying in the Word and believing it to the fullest. At times, I found myself in a daze, especially those nights I couldn't sleep for worrying about Junior being locked up. I spoke with my co-pastor, Susie, a lot about the situation and how I was feeling, and she would reassure me that God is still in control and that Junior would be fine. I began to accept what God allowed. It had to happen this way to keep Junior alive.

When we spoke, I maintained my composure as much as I could. Junior said he was ready to come home and that he should have listened to me. He asked me to contact his lawyer to see if she had any new information. Between the visitations, phone calls, lawyer visits, and my job, I was stressed out. My husband advised me to slow down, but I explained that when you have a loved one in the system, you're their eyes and ears and keep them from being mistreated and misrepresented.

While Junior's lawyer worked to either get the charges against him dropped or secure probation, Junior grew frustrated with the process. I told him that he needed to pray and trust God more than ever, so he started attending church service and Bible study…and he accepted the Lord as his savior! My heart was overwhelmed with joy! As the months passed, Junior got more involved with the Word and built a solid relationship with God. During some of our phone calls, he would even quote scriptures and sing gospel songs.

Six months in, Junior called me frantic because he was being transferred and didn't know why. I immediately notified his lawyer, who said she knew nothing about the move but would check into it. He was transferred to Wichita, Maryland, without any explanation.

The system is a beast, and it's hard to get out without strong family support when you get caught in it. My family helped me research, and we found that the transfer was a mistake, but no one was held accountable for it. We didn't even know who to complain to about it. After all, the system sees black inmates as just another person of color, but my son was suffering. In the meantime, Junior was stabbed by someone in the new location, but he refused to tell who did it. Inmates have the same code as the streets: snitches get stitches. After he was injured, Junior was transferred back to the jail in D.C.

I had to remind Junior constantly that he was never alone; when he felt weak, God was his strength; and when he felt afraid, to remember God's word! I reminded him of *Psalm 46:1-2 NIV — "God is our refuge and strength, an ever-present help in trouble. Therefore we will not fear, though the earth gives way and the mountains fall into the heart of the sea."*

After a year of being locked up, Junior found out he was allegedly a suspect in a case in Maryland. I was shattered once again. The lawyer confirmed this information and advised me that Maryland authorities would pick up Junior and transport him back to face charges there. She had no clue what was happening and had no paperwork with details. Junior was furious.

I couldn't visit Junior at the new facility as often because their process was different, but we spoke by phone. I called my co-pastor, Susie Owens, explaining our dilemma.

"You are a praying mother," she said, "and woman of faith. Your son is going to be alright. I will be praying, as well."

And she did. No matter the day or hour, First Lady Owens was always in my corner.

I notified Mr. Grant, Junior's mentor from the church's youth ministry, of his seemingly impossible situation. Without hesitating, he asked what he could do to help. Then I reached out to Youth Pastor Will, who asked what he could do, as well. I asked them to attend some of the court proceedings in Maryland since I might not have been able to make them all. The enemy tried his hardest to keep me down, but I knew God had me. "Faith over fear," I constantly repeated as my mantra.

It did my heart well to hear Junior say, "I know God is with me, Ma, and I read my Bible every day."

With tears of joy and renewed hope for my child, I said to him, "It took you being incarcerated to finally see your worth."

Then I told him to read *Lamentations 3:22 (KJV): "It is of the Lord's mercies that we are not consumed, because his compassions fails not. They are new every morning: great is thy faithfulness."*

It felt like an eternity that Junior had been locked up, but he was hanging in there, reading the Word, and focusing on how he would change his life around when he was released. But one night, he called upset because they were trying to give him more time. I couldn't go and speak to the lawyer much because of where his office was located, and our schedules wouldn't allow us to connect easily. There was also client-lawyer confidentiality to consider.

Junior's frustration intensified, and I reached out to Mr. Grant and Pastor Will to see if they would be able to attend the next court date. Thankfully, they did. The lawyer filed a motion to have a continuance to get better prepared for the case, which came across his desk last minute. He hadn't had time to prepare or research all the evidence. Junior requested another lawyer to represent him, and we quickly found one. Things looked grim, but I told God I wouldn't complain.

The court proceedings wore heavily on everyone, especially me. It didn't seem like things were working for our good, but I believed God had a plan to bring Junior out. Every time we spoke, I assured him that God would not have brought him this far to fail him. I told him that the Word of God is alive and infused with power to give hope, joy, and peace when all seems lost.

October 2016 was approaching, and the lawyer told Junior the evidence being presented against him was not enough to hold or charge him. In other words, the case against him was looking very weak. I told Junior that God's promise for his life was prevailing despite his situation and circumstances.

With another hearing scheduled for February 2017, I began praying and calling on the prayer warriors that I knew.

I had been in contact with a mother named Arleen, who knew all too well about the court system and having a child in prison. We would speak and pray on the phone for hours during this place of heartbrokenness in my life. She encouraged me to no end and believed with me what God had promised over Junior's life. It had been a long road, but the light was beginning to shine in Junior's favor.

On the day of the hearing, it was decided to keep Junior in custody due to new evidence, but his lawyer believed it was not relevant to the case and would not stick.

The new court date was set for June. In my spirit, I believed this would be the last one. I knew I wouldn't get to the courthouse by the start of the hearing, so I had a group of family and friends to attend in my place until I was able to get there. When I finally arrived, everyone was standing in the hallway.

"It's over. They dropped all the charges," Pastor Will told me.

"Thank you, Jesus," I screamed, then thanked everyone who came to show their support.

Junior had to be processed out, which would take a while. So, we left. When he called later that evening, we went back to pick him up.

Irene Reyes-Smith

"Mom, I'm free!" he hollered.
"Thank God," I said.
"You got that right," Junior proclaimed.

The Badge

These are some of the ways people view the badge that men and women wear. They sometimes forget officers are human.

T = Trust   **B** = Bold
H = Help   **A** = Admired
E = Enemy   **D** = Demanding
                         G = Guidance
                         E = Engaged

Torn: My Badge vs. My Son

Being a police officer was challenging, but I made it through. Helping individuals through their issues, struggles, pain, and views of life is like no one can imagine if you don't walk in an officer's shoes. The struggle is REAL! Not a day went by without me praying for God to protect me, my family, and my co-workers. My biggest challenge was dealing with Junior's behavior. I worked as an officer of the law—a job I wanted since I was a child, but my son fought the law. I remained in my career because I enjoyed helping people, despite opposition from my son. I believed God ordained my footsteps for such a time as this, in this career path He chose for me. I had to put on my shoes of peace to continue on the journey set before me.

The life of a law enforcement officer is different than any other career. You have to know you are the one for the job without a shadow of a doubt—the situations, issues, stress, and many oppositions. The career will have you feeling lonely at times, especially with the situations and circumstances you endure day in and day out, not knowing who to turn to or talk with.

The decision I made to stay wasn't easy, but I had to make it. I let my son know he would have to make better choices, as well. No one is exempt from temptation, and evil is always lurking. How we handle our choices is what makes us. I was there at every hearing, court date, and trial my son had, not knowing what would become of it, but I knew God had a plan and purpose for Junior's life.

"This is my command—be strong and courageous! Do not be afraid or discouraged. For the Lord your God is with you wherever you go." (Joshua 1:9, NLT)

As a mother and an officer, I was determined my son's issues were not going to defeat or break me. I had done my best to keep him safe and uphold the law.

One evening while sitting in the house, I received a call from a detective stating Junior needed to turn himself in. This couldn't be happening again! I immediately called my husband, who calmed me down and said it might not be as bad as I thought. Of course, Junior panicked when I told him.

"I haven't been doing anything," he said.

I believe in karma. When we think life is great and we're doing well, evil is always nearby. I told Junior not to worry, but it was one situation after another with him. One of the hardest things to do is have your child turn himself in, but I knew it was the right thing to do. His father accompanied him and was advised the situation stemmed from the days when Junior was running the streets. Ultimately, he spent a weekend in jail and was back home.

Junior's lifestyle taught him a hard lesson, but he became a better person and drew closer to God. One evening during my meditation time, this scripture jumped in my spirit: *"Train up a child in the way he should go, and when he is old he will not depart from it." (Proverbs 22:6, NKJV)*

The benefits of bringing up children in the Lord are innumerable: they learn victorious power and triumphant living; God will teach them about hope and faith; that no matter how great the trial, they can still put their hope and trust in Him. God has provided the strength to carry children through life's trials, no matter how painful. On the path that God wanted me to travel, I was determined not to be distressed, distracted, or disengaged, which meant I couldn't give up. Despite what was going on with my son, God was my confidence.

"Trust in the Lord with all your heart, and lean not on your own understanding; in all your ways acknowledge Him, and He shall direct your paths." (Proverbs 3:5-6, NKJV)

Keeping this scripture in my heart, I moved forward on God's Word, which never failed me. He expected me to be diligent, hardworking, and fulfill my purpose to serve Him and His children with good works.

Irene Reyes-Smith

I remained focused and asked for help to navigate my journey because the tricks, schemes, and plots of the enemy tried to make me throw in the towel. But I thank God for the victory over His plan. *Proverbs 13:4 (NLT)* reminded me, *"Lazy people want much but get little, but those who work hard will prosper."*

God told me that my work is to serve the community and draw lost souls closer to Him. My job is to protect and serve; God is a protector, and all work is done for His purpose and glory. I remember saying to myself, "My son is the seed God allowed me to birth." Therefore, Junior wasn't going to fail. He was in the hands of the Lord.

A mother wants the best for her child, but if we fail to allow them to grow into themselves and constantly bail them out of their mistakes, we can damage them without realizing it. Some people may think I was crazy for staying on the job, but God never failed me. If we obey and follow His direction, God always makes a way.

The Finale

After everything I have shared with you, you may be wondering what's going on with me now. Well, I'm still working, God is in control, and my journey has enabled me to assist other mothers with their sons.

All the long nights, court dates, trials, hospital and jail visits, heartaches, pain, stress, triumphs, and tribulations were all for a reason much bigger than me. Throughout my career, I have encountered single mothers and parents of adolescents who were dealing with the same issues I did with Junior. I offered practical advice, information, words of comfort, and prayer to each one. I have guided youth and helped families deal with their rebellion. I am so glad God trusted me with this task.

Junior is doing well, and we are closer than ever. He has enrolled in a vocational school to get his diploma, and I'm so very proud of him! He isn't totally where he wants to be, but it's a start. I'm praying God continues to order his footsteps and help him become the man He wants him to be. Transformation changes us from the inside out. I have to believe that, especially in times when I wonder if I failed my son.

"You did your best," God assured me.

In these last days, the devil is waging war against our children, knowing they are the leaders of the future. That is why I constantly prayed and sought deliverance from bondage for my children. One of the most effective ways to deliver a child is to pray over them as they sleep, in gentleness and love. Prayer always helped my children. They weren't perfect; however, prayer helped protect them from the evil that could have plagued their lives. My son is home, and I am at peace. However, that's only the beginning of our next journey.

The system is what we make it. I have learned so much about democracy and the American dream during Junior's incarceration. His job search, registering in school, and rejoining society have been a harsh reality, but he is working hard to make it all happen. At times, he grows frustrated, but I reassure him that God doesn't make mistakes. He brought Junior out to prove that He is the author and finisher of our faith; He wants Junior to know He is in complete control of everything concerning him.

Junior lived with me for a while, that is until he decided to do his own thing and set his own rules. Not in my house. He ended up moving in with another family member, which was the best decision for both of us. Although I was hurt, I remained calm and gave it to God. I reminded Junior that the road might be rough, but God will help him endure if he stays the course. He needed to know that all things are possible with God, and Jesus was granting him a second chance to exalt Him.

Junior is taking life more seriously and transforming for the better. I am overjoyed how God has rekindled the relationship between my husband and son, too. Nothing is too hard with God on your side—even bringing the two men in my life together in peace. Look at God!

If there's anyone who is going through this situation, know that you are not alone. Prayer works and never fails us. Stay committed, connected, and don't compromise your self-worth because of external pressure and internal struggles. We can't do anything of value apart from the Lord.

When we lay down our plans and accept God's plans for our lives, we exchange pride for the peace of God. For anything to work, God has to be part of it.

I Am a SURVIVOR

S = I found **Safety** in the Lord

U = **Unity**

R = **Regained** control over my life

V = I am **Victorious**

I = **Imagine** all possibilities with God on our side

V = Your **Voice**, **Value,** and **Victories**

O = **Open** to possibilities

R = **Restoration** has taken place

My Survival

My survival wasn't easy, but I persevered. I can do all things through Christ who strengthens me. God reminded me that we are here to serve. It's not just a job but an assignment from Him. His Word says, *"For many are called, but few are chosen." (Matthew 22:14 NLT)* I am chosen to serve as a soldier in the army of the Lord, to keep peace in the community, and to serve here on Earth.

God doesn't make mistakes; only we do. When we don't adhere to His Word, we become overwhelmed and stressed. I often felt like I was suffocating because, to some degree, I believed my life was under subjection for my disobedience to surrender Junior to Jesus.

I wanted to rescue my son, but his life was not mine to fix. As parents, we all want the best for our children, but we must allow God to order their footsteps as He knows best. Children are a gift from God, but God instructs us to train them up in the way they should go. Years of crying, worrying, and frustration took a toll on me, but I knew in order to survive, I couldn't allow the enemy to keep me in bondage or use my son to plague my life.

Even as people looked down on me and my circumstances, God was the head of my life. I kept pressing, praising, and dwelling on God's promises for my family and me.

"It is of the Lord's mercies that we are not consumed, because his compassions fail not. They are new every morning: great is thy faithfulness." (Lamentations 3:22-23, KJV)

God was with me, even when I didn't feel He was. I had to stop doubting myself and believing everything was my fault. When kids think they are grown enough to do adult things, they will try you — no matter how you raised them. Parenting books and classes are abundant, but as parents, we have to rely on God's Word. His Word is true. We must be open and transparent with ourselves about ourselves and our lives.

I have this saying: "Until you are tired of being sick and tired, you will continue to operate the same way." Upon examining myself, I wondered if I was living the life God had predestined for me. If so, was I living up to His expectations of it? What could I have done differently? I didn't have any definitive answers, but if nothing else, I can say I learned to depend on God's Word and spend more time in His presence. The test, trials, tribulations, and testimonies were all part of His plan and purpose for me.

My determination prevailed as I worked with at-risk youth. Life is hard and has its times of hurt, but it's okay to ask for help when it is needed. There is nothing to be ashamed of if your child has been in trouble, acting out of control, or is not the best in school. Do not let feelings of guilt make you think you owe them the world.

"Children, obey your parents in the Lord, for this is right." (Ephesians 6:1, NIV)

As parents, we strive for excellence in raising our children, but sometimes pride, ego, self-righteousness, and believing we have it all together gets in the way. The world makes us feel that everything has to be a certain way of living, but the only way is God's way. After all, He wants the best for our children and us. He created us all in His image (which was good in His sight). All He requires us to do is trust Him, accept Him, and believe.

The enemy is a liar and deceiver who wants our children to be defiant, out of control, and disobedient. But the Bible declares for children to honor their father and mother, which is the first commandment with promise.

"Children, obey your parents in the Lord [that is, accept their guidance and discipline as His representatives], for this is right [for obedience teaches wisdom and self-discipline]. HONOR [esteem, value as precious] YOUR FATHER AND YOUR MOTHER [and be respectful to them]—this is the first commandant with a promise—SO THAT IT MAY BE WELL WITH YOU, AND THAT YOU MAY HAVE A LONG LIFE ON THE EARTH." (Ephesians 6:1-3, AMP)

The enemy knows the Word of God, too, as he walked with Him but wanted more power. Although we don't all have the same story, situation, or suffer the same adversity, I do know there is only one God. Our God wants us to have a purpose-filled life and give willingly and sacrificially for the betterment of others despite what we have been through. God always gets the glory because the battle belongs to Him, but the victory belongs to me.

God is enough. He has all power to deliver us from our troubles, as long as we believe.

I survived because I did not give up and asked for help, which our Heavenly Father wants us to do. When we face trials, tribulations, tragedies, and turmoil, God is there waiting for us to come to Him. Because I went to Him, I survived, and so can you. Everything we experience is sometimes from the Lord's hand to see if we will call on Him.

No matter what career you choose, remember that no one is exempt from the pressures of life, the pain and hurt from loved ones, and the attacks of the enemy. I had to fight using the Armor of God—the sword of the Spirit, the belt of truth, and the helmet of salvation (my mind). I had to flood my mind with Christ-centered thoughts. The enemy wants us to have doubt, fear, and turn away from Jesus, but we serve a God can do exceedingly, abundantly above all that we could ever imagine.

"If you remain in me and my words remain in you, ask whatever you wish, and it will be given you." (John 15:7, NIV)

I pray this book has been a blessing to your mind and soul. God knows the steps we take; He's there with open arms to grace us with His love and mercy. I hope I have also shared some insight on how we are not alone; it takes a village. God is always with us and will never leave nor forsake us.

Writing this book and sharing what I have been through has been healing for me. God knew I had to birth this book for my healing and His deliverance over me. My purpose is what kept me. The trials, tribulations, and tasks I have endured made me the woman I am today.

I leave you with this: The Bible encourages us in many ways not to give up. Always pray and put God first in your life. *Galatians 6:9 (KJV)* says, *"And let us not be weary in well doing: for in due season we shall reap, if we faint not."* We have many seasons in our lives, and they are given by God to strength and encourage us along our paths. There is no way every season in our lives is going to be easy, but with great faith and God on our side, we will win, and it won't end hard. But God!

Acknowledgements

I want to take this time to recognize and give God thanks for my husband Dion, my love and Boaz, for everything you are to me and for staying by my side through it all. It wasn't easy, but it was worth the long nights and countless hours on the computer. You hung in there and believed with me in my vision for this project that God gave me. I couldn't have done it without you. I love you endlessly.

To my children, the inspiration of my life and for me writing this book. Times weren't always good, but we made it, and I love you so much for your support. I know there was apprehension in the beginning, but y'all are the best. Mom loves you.

To my family for trusting and believing I could accomplish this chapter of my life, for never giving up on me, and for always having my back. Thank you for being in my corner and cheering me on.

My bishop and co-pastor, Owens, for the teaching, leadership, mentoring, and love shown to me during the

Irene Reyes-Smith

tragic times in my life. Thank you for guiding and helping me keep the faith in God, no matter what.

My best friends, Lisa and Tiffany, who were there through my darkest hours, staying in my corner and cheering me on.

To Ma Arleen and the church members who prayed and believed God with me.

To my niece in Christ, Kiawana Leaf, who motivated and pointed me in the right direction to write this book. I love you always.

To my co-workers who had my best interest and never judged or looked down on me.

To Pen Legacy LLC for your guidance throughout this publishing experience, seeing my vision, and helping me make it all come true.

CPSIA information can be obtained
at www.ICGtesting.com
Printed in the USA
LVHW022019240521
688348LV00015B/703